The Greatest Name on Earth!

from
⋙ PSALM 8 ⋘

by Joel Anderson
illustrated by Kristi Carter & Joel Anderson

A Golden Book • New York
Golden Books Publishing Company, Inc.
New York, New York 10106

Dedicated to Rachel Ann Beery, age 7,
and her family, Mark, Laura, & Matthew Beery

O Lord, our Lord, how majestic is Your Name
in all the earth!…What is man that You are mindful of him,
the son of man that You care for him?
Psalm 8:1,4

"When we found out about Rachel's brain tumor,
a pineoblastoma, we began a walk of complete faith and trust
in God that not many people experience. We take comfort
in knowing God cares for His most valuable creation."

Scripture for dedication taken from the HOLY BIBLE, NEW INTERNATIONAL VERSION. Copyright © 1973, 1978, 1984 by International Bible Society. Used by permission of Zondervan Publishing House.

O Lord, how excellent is Your name.

Your name is the greatest one on Earth!
Your glory shines from Heaven.

From the lips of children and babies come sounds of praise.

When I look into the sky
at night and see the work
of Your fingers . . .

I think to myself,
"I am so small."

You have made so many people.
But You know us all,
and You care for each of us.

You have made us beautiful like the angels.
You crown us with glory and honor!

You let us take care
of Your creations—
the flocks and herds, . . .

the wild animals, . . .

the birds in the air, . . .

and the fish in the sea.

O Lord . . .

how excellent is Your name.

It's the greatest name on Earth!